After-school FUN

Art Classes

by JoAnn Early Macken

Reading consultant: Susan Nations, M.Ed., author/literacy coach/consultant

WR WEEKLY READER
EARLY LEARNING LIBRARY

Please visit our web site at: www.earlyliteracy.cc
For a free color catalog describing Weekly Reader® Early Learning Library's list
of high-quality books, call 1-877-445-5824 (USA) or 1-800-387-3178 (Canada).
Weekly Reader® Early Learning Library's fax: (414) 336-0164.

Library of Congress Cataloging-in-Publication Data

Macken, JoAnn Early, 1953-
    Art classes / by JoAnn Early Macken.
      p. cm. — (After-school fun)
    Includes bibliographical references and index.
    ISBN 0-8368-4511-0 (lib. bdg.)
    ISBN 0-8368-4518-8 (softcover)
    1. Art—Study and teaching (Elementary)—United States—
Juvenile literature. I. Title.
N362.M33   2005
372.5′044—dc22   2004043115

This edition first published in 2005 by
Weekly Reader® Early Learning Library
330 West Olive Street, Suite 100
Milwaukee, WI 53212 USA

Copyright © 2005 by Weekly Reader® Early Learning Library

Photographer: Gregg Andersen
Picture research: Diane Laska-Swanke
Art direction and page layout: Tammy West

Printed in the United States of America

1 2 3 4 5 6 7 8 9 09 08 07 06 05

Note to Educators and Parents

Reading is such an exciting adventure for young children! They are beginning to integrate their oral language skills with written language. To encourage children along the path to early literacy, books must be colorful, engaging, and interesting; they should invite the young reader to explore both the print and the pictures.

After-School Fun is a new series designed to help children read about the kinds of activities they enjoy in their free time. In each book, young readers learn about a different artistic endeavor, physical activity, or learning experience.

Each book is specially designed to support the young reader in the reading process. The familiar topics are appealing to young children and invite them to read — and reread — again and again. The full-color photographs and enhanced text further support the student during the reading process.

In addition to serving as wonderful picture books in schools, libraries, homes, and other places where children learn to love reading, these books are specifically intended to be read within an instructional guided reading group. This small group setting allows beginning readers to work with a fluent adult model as they make meaning from the text. After children develop fluency with the text and content, the book can be read independently. Children and adults alike will find these books supportive, engaging, and fun!

— Susan Nations, M.Ed., author, literacy coach,
and consultant in literacy development

After school, I go to art class. I always wear my art shirt. My other clothes stay clean.

In art class, we learn about colors. We draw with crayons. We draw self-portraits. My self-portrait is a picture of me.

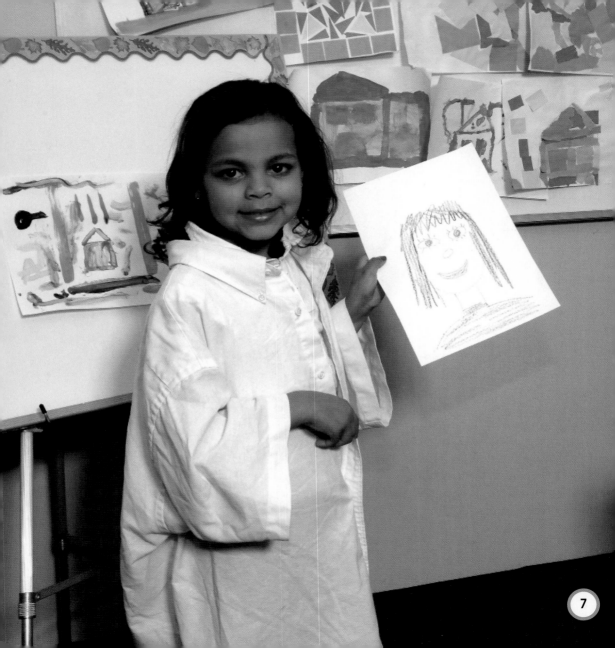

Art can be messy. Before class, we cover the tables. Paper keeps the tables clean.

We learn about lines.
We paint with brushes.
We paint thick lines
and thin lines. We
paint our homes.

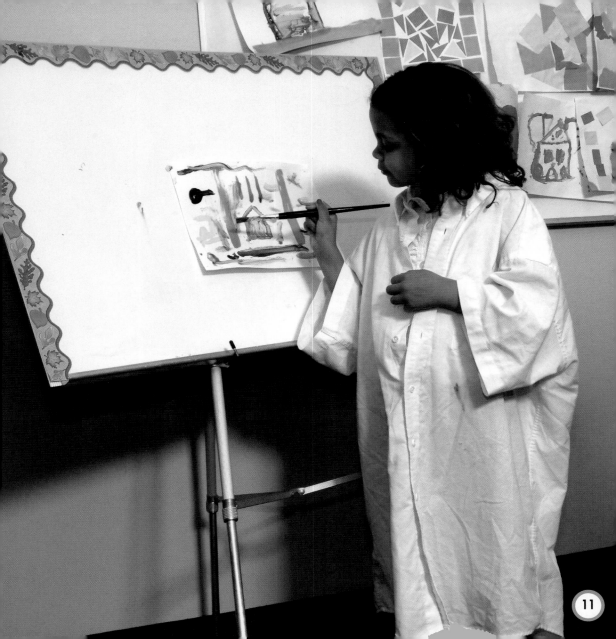

We learn about shapes. We make collages. We make them from colored paper. They look like windows.

We learn about forms. We make papier-mâché monsters. Mine has purple ears.

We learn about texture.
We make clay pots. We
make them from long
rolls of clay.

We always clean up after class. We wipe off the tables. We put our supplies away.

Our art is on display!
Look what we made!

Glossary

collages — art made from different materials glued onto surfaces

form — something with three dimensions that takes up space

line — a continuing mark on a surface

papier-mâché — a molding material made of paper, glue, and water

shape — something with two dimensions that contains space

texture — the feeling of a surface

For More Information

Books

Color. How Artists Use (series). Paul Flux (Heinemann Library)

More Than Meets The Eye: Seeing Art with All Five Senses. Bob Raczka (Millbrook)

Oxford First Book of Art. Gillian Wolfe (Oxford University Press)

The Art Box. Gail Gibbons (Holiday House)

Web Sites

Artist's Toolkit

www.artsconnected.org/toolkit/
Explore the tools that artists use — such as line, color, and balance — to build works of art

Index

About the Author

JoAnn Early Macken is the author of two rhyming picture books, *Sing-Along Song* and *Cats on Judy*, and six other series of nonfiction books for beginning readers. Her poems have appeared in several children's magazines. A graduate of the M.F.A. in Writing for Children and Young Adults program at Vermont College, she lives in Wisconsin with her husband and their two sons. Visit her Web site at www.joannmacken.com.